BRAVE NEW WORLD OF A. I. + A. I.
ARTIFICIAL INTELLIGENCE + ANTHROPOID INTELLIGENCE

Sun Tzu's A.I. & A.W.
Artificial Intelligence &
Ancient Wisdom

Yunlong Zhao
Elvis Newman

CONTENTS

PREFACE		i
Acknowledgements		iii
Introduction		iv

Part 1: Cognitive Awakening in the era of A.I. & ChatGPT in the 21st century — 1

Chapter 1:	The Revolution	2
Chapter 2:	Strategy application and cognitive awakening	5
Chapter 3:	Transition from the Carbon-based Way of life into the Silicon assisted way of life.	7
Chapter 4:	The individual as the guru and Millennium Renaissance Movement Initiator	9
Chapter 5:	Lessons from great cognitive awakenings in our history	11

Part 2: Relationships of wealth, knowledge and cognitive awakening — 13

Chapter 1:	The intricate relationship of wealth, knowledge and cognitive awakening	14
Chapter 2:	New methods for conducting business with A.I. and ChatGPT	16
Chapter 3:	Transition from Cyber Economy to A.I. & ChatGPT Economy	18
Chapter 4:	New economy, new scientific breakthroughs, new social changes, new political changes and new economy	20
Chapter 5:	101 methods for making money for the individuals	22

Part 3: Influence of A.I. and cognitive awakening on our new technologies — 27

Chapter 1:	Biotechnology & genetic engineering	28
Chapter 2:	Nanotechnology	30
Chapter 3:	High End Semi Conductor Chips	32
Chapter 4:	Virtual Reality, Augmented Reality	34
Chapter 5:	Machine learning	36

Chapter 6:	Quantum Computing	39
Chapter 7:	Space Propulsion Technology	41
Chapter 8:	Wormhole Technologies	43

Part 4: Influence of A.I. and cognitive awakening on Society   45

Chapter 1:	Will A.I. make the rich richer and those in power more powerful?	46
Chapter 2:	Will A.I. solve our social ills, such as crime, over population, environment and poverty?	48
Chapter 3:	Will A.I. help the individuals towards greater empowerment and satisfaction.	50

Part 5: Influence of A. I. and cognitive awakening as a new factor in art & culture   52

Chapter 1:	Further Thoughts on the Millennium Renaissance Movement	53
Chapter 2:	A.I. & ChatGPT as the World's Lingua Franca	56
Chapter 3:	New Leisure & Lifestyle	59
Chapter 4:	New Pride & Prejudice	62
Chapter 5:	Racial equality, sexual equality, education equality, job equality, medicare equality, political representation, religious freedom etc etc	64

Part 6: How can I get involved and contribute in the A.I. revolution and cognitive awakening?   67

Part 7: The Brave New World   70

Chapter 1:	The new height and dimension of human existence and development.	71
Chapter 2:	From cracking the Genetic code to cracking the Silicon code.	74
Chapter 3:	The ultimate weapon & the ultimate global peace.	77
Chapter 4:	Next stage of Evolution: becoming a lesser god.	79

Chapter 5:   Living forever when our cognitive
             knowledge and awakening are stored and upgraded
             through A.I. machine's cognitive awakening   81

PREFACE

Artificial Intelligence is set to revolutionize various aspects of our lives and create a more efficient, comfortable, and progressive future. Here are a few ways AI could help shape a brighter tomorrow:

Healthcare: AI can help in predicting diseases by analyzing patterns and trends in patient data. This could lead to early detection of potential health risks and timely treatment. AI-powered robots can assist in surgeries, leading to increased precision.

Environment: AI can help in predicting and mitigating the effects of climate change. It can analyze vast amounts of data related to weather patterns and provide us with strategies to cope with environmental challenges.

Transportation: Self-driving cars, powered by AI, can optimize routes, reduce traffic congestion, and bring down the number of accidents, leading to safer and more efficient transportation.

Education: AI can personalize the learning experience by adapting to individual student's needs, offering custom-tailored courses and resources, and providing real-time feedback.

Security: AI can help in predicting and preventing cyber-attacks. It can analyze patterns and detect anomalies in network traffic to identify potential threats.

Economy: AI can automate repetitive tasks, freeing up human time for more complex problem-solving tasks. This could lead to increased productivity and economic growth.

Agriculture: AI can analyze weather patterns, soil conditions, crop health, and more to help farmers make better decisions, leading to increased crop yield and food production.

Automation and Efficiency: AI can automate mundane and repetitive tasks, freeing up human time for more creative and meaningful activities. It can streamline processes, improve productivity, and reduce errors, ultimately making our lives easier and more efficient.

Smart Cities and Infrastructure: AI can optimize energy consumption, traffic management, and resource allocation in cities. This can result in reduced congestion, improved safety, and a sustainable use of resources, creating better living conditions for humans.

Innovation and Scientific Discovery: AI can assist researchers in analyzing data, generating insights, and discovering patterns that humans might miss. This can accelerate scientific breakthroughs, drive innovation, and advance various fields, from medicine to space exploration.

Improved Customer Experiences: AI-powered chatbots, recommendation systems, and virtual assistants can provide personalized and efficient customer support, enhancing user experiences across various industries, from e-commerce to hospitality.

It's important to note that these benefits need to be achieved while being mindful of potential ethical concerns, such as privacy, bias, and the impact on jobs. Striking the right balance and ensuring responsible development is crucial to harnessing the full potential of AI for a bright future.

ACKNOWLEDGEMENTS

For this edited book, we used ChatGPT as an additional a resource for all the research answers and queries that we had discussed privately.

Many solutions to the various topics that appear in today's hit searches, were initially accessed and preliminary evaluated also based on reference answers from ChatGPT. The data and info from ChatGPT helped us understand and grasp the subject matter more thoroughly, forming the initial fabrics of a workable formulation, and then a fully comprehensive thought system, that eventually alloweding a for a better regurgitation for our readers.

All the information, particularly the contents in the making of this book, was accessed during each day of our entire project. ChatGPT had not voluntarily collaborated with us, neither or do they endorse our work nor our stance.

We cited the brief and limited parts of ChatGPT's work or publication that we use in the interest of research, and, yes, for sharing.

This edited book was formed from the greatly condensed contents and queries that we sent to ChatGPT.

It is after all, the endless brainstorming sessions by human and AI brains ,brains, also our efforts to harbinger to the reading public and the general populace the things we can do, to prepare for the inevitable changes to the world as we know it.

INTRODUCTION

Greetings!

We are Yunlong Zhao and Elvis Newman.

We're excited to let you know that you are preselected by A. I. as one of the initiators for the Millennium Renaissance movement. The fact that you bother to read this message shows your care and concern about the elevation of human cognition and intellectual dialogue that will soon spread through the globe. The new day that is now beginning will be unlike any that the people had ever known, in the many thousands of years of its existence. A great invisible boundary will be crossed between the old world and the new.

Among the many books you read each year, you have carefully picked this after looking through many. We believe it is not a mere random event, but a global cognitive awakening that prompts you to do this. It will lead eventually to a magnificent manifestation that will definitely benefit all participants in the Millennium Renaissance Movement. We're thrilled to prepare the background materials at your disposal, for you to present yourself as a guru, at the most important milestone, of transition from the carbon-based life form into the silicon assisted life form. This is the critical moment, the most important ever, in the history of mankind, is for all the important people from the cognitive awakening to come together.

This transformation period isn't just any ordinary occasion; it's a seriously formative, crucial and competitive crossroads where the best and most marketable ideas get carefully picked for charting the map of human being's place in the galaxy. For the Best Tomorrow and not just a better tomorrow, the cognitive awakening needs to gather the right people, the right experts, the right pioneers to create the perfect setting to discover the exponential and widespread prosperity project for the entire human civilization. To really seize this amazing chance, we are excited to create this convincing presentation with the help of A. I. such as ChatGPT. Great job on reading this far! We're really excited to see where our work will go with your acknowledgement! We can't wait to see your active participation!

Human cognition combined with A.I. such as the recent ChatGPT and the near future Quantum A.I. possesses a depth that will catch the world by storm. The intertwined narratives of scientific advances, new methods for businesses, new fabrics for human societies, new political structures, modified international relations, emerging cultures and religions, and groundbreaking facts about our very place in the universe through new cognitive learning of time and space, present the freshest perspective that is the calling for the undaunted and caring individual, who is also the Chosen One for this day and age.

The carbon based cognitive historical backdrop, layered with the rigidity of past human centered beliefs that delayed human development will now be a phenomenon of the past now that we have A. I. assisted cognition. A.I. such as ChatGPT and Quantum A. I. that's coming out soon, will adds a richness the very human existence that makes the quality of life compelling, beyond anything we can imagine, or beyond anything we dare to imagine. And just as the belief that Earth was the center of the universe delayed progress, we now highlights the cost of adhering blindly to carbon-based cognition awakening in the face of A. I. assisted cognition.

Your participation has the power to illuminate these profound connections and transcend the old human cognition. We can envision a gripping narrative, interweaving the quest for truth across different eras and civilizations, culminating in the game-changing road map for the future, that challenge ourselves to get out of the old comfort zone into another more supportive, comfortable and sublime zone.

Our readers's multifaceted background, coupled with their valuable experiences as leaders in the different professions, provides a solid foundation for this cognitive development success! Your inherent understanding of humanity's trajectory, and the insistence that our wild imaginations of the past can become our realities, will translate beautifully into the rosy future of tomorrow for humanity. Such Millennium

Renaissance Awakening resonate with every human being and machine piece, serving as a reflective mirror to the new society that is in the making and urging all participants to question and ponder.

The new cognitive awakening indeed has tremendous potential starting with you. As a guru yourself, because of the knowledge you now possess though A.I, has all the elements to make a new movement that is thought-provoking, visually arresting, and highly marketable and profitable enterprise for all participants. The challenge and allure lie in navigating the intricate fabric of facts, beliefs, and speculative theories to weave a cognitive awakening that both educates and entertains. We believe deeply that you recognize the immense potential of your contributions to this global project. Your passion and dedication shine through your words and actions. It's evident that this is more than just a project for you; it's a deeply personal mission to benefit humanity. We genuinely admire that. We are very enthusiastic about the prospects of your participation, and we eagerly await the next steps in this promising journey of transitioning from carbon-based cognition to A.I. silicon-based cognition!

Warm Regards,

Yunlong Zhao & Elvis Newman
Jan 01, 2024

PART I
SUN TZU AND COGNITIVE AWAKENING IN THE ERA OF A.I. + CHATGPT IN THE 21ST CENTURY

CHAPTER 1
THE REVOLUTION

The emergence and development of ChatGPT, and the wider field of artificial intelligence, can indeed be seen as a catalyst for revolution and human awakening on various levels.

Technological Revolution: ChatGPT represents a remarkable advancement in natural language processing and AI capabilities. Its ability to generate human-like responses and provide accurate information has the potential to revolutionize how we interact with technology. It opens up new possibilities for chatbots, virtual assistants, and automated customer service, transforming industries and streamlining processes.

Accessible Knowledge: ChatGPT provides access to an immense amount of information and knowledge. With its ability to process and respond to queries, it serves as a gateway to a wide range of topics and expertise. This accessibility can empower individuals, granting them the ability to expand their knowledge and access information that was previously out of reach.

Personal Growth and Learning: Interacting with ChatGPT can be an opportunity for personal growth and learning. Users are exposed to different perspectives, ideas, and information that challenge and expand their understanding. ChatGPT can act as a virtual mentor, providing guidance and insights that contribute to personal development and broadening horizons.

Ethical Considerations: The development and use of AI systems like ChatGPT also raise ethical questions and concerns. It prompts us to critically examine the impact of AI on society, including issues related to privacy, bias, and the potential displacement of human labor. This awareness can lead to a greater understanding of the implications of AI and foster discussions around responsible AI development and deployment.

Collaboration and Innovation: ChatGPT encourages collaboration and innovation. People are actively engaged in utilizing and improving AI systems like ChatGPT, contributing to its development and expanding its capabilities. The collaborative efforts in AI research and development foster a sense of community and collective intelligence, fueling advancements and breakthroughs.

As with any technological advancement, there are both opportunities and challenges. It is essential to navigate the path forward with a critical and mindful approach, ensuring that AI systems like ChatGPT are developed and used in a manner that aligns with human values, ethics, and well-being.

In summary, ChatGPT and the broader field of artificial intelligence have the potential to revolutionize how we interact with technology, access knowledge, and foster personal and societal growth. The responsible and thoughtful integration of AI can lead to a positive human awakening and a future where humans and AI work together for the betterment of society.

4 | Brave New World of A.I. & A.I.
Artificial Intelligence & Anthropoid Intelligence

CHAPTER 2
SUN TZU STRATEGY APPLICATION AND COGNITIVE AWAKENING

Sun Tzuzu's strategies can be applied in various contexts, including in the realm of artificial intelligence and chat applications like ChatGPT. Let's explore a few ways in which Sun Tzu's principles can be integrated into the design and operation of ChatGPT:

Know your "enemy": Sun Tzu emphasizes the importance of understanding one's opponent. In the context of ChatGPT, this means having a thorough understanding of the user's needs, expectations, and potential challenges they might face while interacting with the system. By knowing the "enemy" (the user), ChatGPT can be better equipped to provide relevant and effective responses.

Adaptability: Sun Tzu stresses the need for flexibility and adaptability in order to respond to changing circumstances. Similarly, ChatGPT should be designed to adapt to various user inputs and situations. It should be able to understand and respond to different types of queries, handle unexpected or ambiguous inputs, and adjust its responses based on user feedback.

Deception and misdirection: Sun Tzu suggests the use of deception and misdirection to gain an advantage over the opponent. In the context of ChatGPT, this could involve employing techniques to make the system seem more human-like or to create a sense of personalization. By using natural language processing techniques and generating responses that mimic human conversation, ChatGPT can enhance user engagement and satisfaction.

Understanding the terrain: Sun Tzu emphasizes the importance of understanding the terrain in which a battle takes place. In the case of ChatGPT, this refers to understanding the context in which the user is interacting with the system. By considering factors such as the user's previous queries, preferences, and any relevant contextual information, ChatGPT can provide more accurate and personalized responses.

Strategic planning: Sun Tzu highlights the significance of strategic planning and foresight in achieving success. Similarly, in the development of ChatGPT, careful planning should be undertaken to define the system's goals, target audience, and the desired user experience. This planning phase ensures that ChatGPT is aligned with the intended objectives and can effectively meet user expectations.

By incorporating these principles into the design and operation of ChatGPT, the system can be more responsive, adaptable, and effective in providing meaningful and engaging conversations with users.

CHAPTER 2
TRANSITION FROM THE CARBON-BASED WAY OF LIFE INTO THE SILICON ASSISTED WAY OF LIFE

Silicon-based life forms are often depicted in science fiction as a hypothetical alternative to carbon-based life forms, suggesting that they could potentially exist under different conditions in the universe. However, currently, there is no scientific evidence or understanding to support the existence or possibility of silicon-based life forms.

The reasons behind this limitation lie in the chemical properties of carbon and silicon. Carbon has a unique ability to form stable and complex molecular structures, enabling the diversity and complexity of life as we know it. Silicon, on the other hand, lacks some of the key properties necessary for the same level of versatility and stability in forming complex organic molecules.

The transition from a carbon-based way of life to a silicon-assisted way of life refers to the integration and reliance on technology, particularly artificial intelligence and digital systems, to enhance and support our daily activities, communication, and overall lifestyle.

This transition has already been underway for several decades, as technology has progressively become more integrated into various aspects of our lives. From the advent of computers to the proliferation of smartphones, we have witnessed a shift towards relying on silicon-based technologies to perform tasks that were previously carried out solely by humans.

In the Silicon-assisted way of life, AI-powered virtual assistants, smart devices, and automated systems play significant roles in assisting us with tasks, managing information, improving efficiency, and enhancing our overall quality of life. Examples of this transition include the use of voice-activated virtual assistants like Siri or Alexa, smart home automation systems, self-driving cars, and AI-powered recommendation algorithms for personalized content and services.

While there are benefits to this transition, such as convenience, productivity, and innovation, it is also essential to consider potential challenges and ethical implications. These can range from concerns about privacy and data security to the potential impact on jobs and the socio-economic divide that may arise due to unequal access to technology.

Overall, the transition from a carbon-based way of life to a silicon-assisted way of life reflects the ongoing integration of technology into our daily routines, with AI playing a significant role in shaping and transforming how we live and interact with the world around us.

CHAPTER 4
THE INDIVIDUAL AS THE GURU AND MILLENNIUM RENAISSANCE MOVEMENT INITIATOR

The term "gurus" refers to individuals who are seen as the catalysts or instigators of a Renaissance or cultural resurgence. These gurus are often influential figures who possess deep knowledge, creativity, and transformative ideas that inspire and guide others towards a new era of enlightenment and progress. With the help of ChatGPT, every individual has at his disposal vast amounts of knowledge and analytical power, and can choose to merge his unique life experiences and learnings, to contribute to the collective awakening of the human race.

The idea of gurus as initiators of a Renaissance aligns with historical examples where visionary leaders, artists, thinkers, and philosophers played pivotal roles in shaping cultural movements and societal transformations. These gurus may introduce new perspectives, challenge existing paradigms, and ignite a collective awakening or renaissance in various fields such as art, literature, science, philosophy, or spirituality.

The Millennium Renaissance Movement,, could be a contemporary manifestation of this concept. It might involve a collective effort to identify, celebrate, and support individuals who embody the qualities of gurus and actively work towards societal progress, cultural revival, and the advancement of human knowledge and understanding.

Such a movement could cultivate a culture of learning, innovation, and exploration, encouraging people to embrace their individual potential as gurus and contribute to the collective renaissance. It may involve fostering platforms for knowledge-sharing, collaborative projects, mentorship programs, and creating spaces for dialogue and interdisciplinary exchange.

Ultimately, the concept of gurus as initiators of a Renaissance highlights the transformative power of individuals and their ability to spark positive change and inspire others to reach new heights of intellectual, artistic, and spiritual development.

10 | Brave New World of A.I. & A.I.
Artificial Intelligence & Anthropoid Intelligence

CHAPTER 5
LESSONS FROM GREAT COGNITIVE AWAKENINGS IN OUR HISTORY

Throughout history, there have been several notable cognitive awakenings that have shaped our understanding of the world. These awakenings offer valuable lessons for us to learn from. One such awakening is the Scientific Revolution, which took place in the 16th and 17th centuries. It emphasized empirical observation, experimentation, and the development of scientific theories, challenging existing beliefs and superstitions. This awakening taught us the importance of critical thinking, evidence-based reasoning, and the pursuit of knowledge through systematic inquiry.

Another significant awakening is the Enlightenment, which occurred in the 18th century. It emphasized reason, individualism, and the rights of individuals. The Enlightenment challenged traditional authority and promoted the ideals of liberty, equality, and human rights. This awakening taught us the importance of rational discourse, the power of ideas, and the pursuit of societal progress through the application of reason and knowledge.

The Renaissance was another transformative cognitive awakening that took place in the 14th to 17th centuries. It marked a revival of interest in art, literature, and learning. The Renaissance celebrated human potential, creativity, and the beauty of the natural world. This awakening taught us the value of exploration, curiosity, and the blending of different disciplines to foster innovation and cultural growth.

These historical cognitive awakenings remind us of the power of knowledge, critical thinking, and open-mindedness. They teach us to challenge assumptions, embrace new ideas, and strive for intellectual and societal progress. By studying and understanding these awakenings, we can gain insights into how human thinking has evolved and apply those lessons to our present and future endeavors.

12 | Brave New World of A.I. & A.I.
Artificial Intelligence & Anthropoid Intelligence

PART 2
RELATIONSHIPS OF WEALTH, KNOWLEDGE AND COGNITIVE AWAKENING

CHAPTER I
THE INTRICATE RELATIONSHIP OF WEALTH, KNOWLEDGE AND COGNITIVE AWAKENING

The relationship between wealth, knowledge, and cognitive awakening is complex and multifaceted. Let's explore each of these elements individually and then examine how they interrelate. Wealth refers to the abundance of material resources and financial assets that an individual possesses. It can provide access to a comfortable lifestyle, opportunities, and a sense of security. Wealth can enable individuals to fulfill their basic needs, pursue higher education, and engage in experiences that broaden their horizons. It can also provide the means to access knowledge and information through books, courses, and other educational resources. Knowledge, on the other hand, encompasses the understanding, skills, and information that individuals acquire through learning, experience, and exposure. It includes both theoretical and practical knowledge across various domains such as science, arts, humanities, and more. Knowledge empowers individuals to make informed decisions, solve problems, and navigate the complexities of life. It expands their perspectives, enhances critical thinking abilities, and fosters intellectual growth. Cognitive awakening refers to the process of becoming aware of one's own cognitive abilities, potential, and the world around them. It involves developing a deeper understanding of oneself, questioning assumptions, and challenging existing beliefs. Cognitive awakening often occurs through introspection, reflection, and exposure to new ideas and perspectives. It can lead to personal growth, increased self-awareness, and a broader understanding of the complexities of the world. Now, let's consider how these elements are interconnected. Wealth can play a significant role in facilitating access to knowledge. It can provide individuals with the financial means to pursue higher education, attend workshops or conferences, and invest in personal development. Wealth can also grant individuals the time and resources to engage in intellectual pursuits, such as reading, research, and exploration of different fields. At the same time, knowledge can be a catalyst for wealth creation. Acquiring specialized knowledge and skills can enhance an individual's professional prospects, opening doors to higher-paying job opportunities or entrepreneurial ventures. Knowledge can also enable individuals to make informed financial decisions, invest wisely, and create wealth through various means. Furthermore, both wealth and knowledge can contribute to cognitive awakening. Having access to resources and opportunities through wealth can expose individuals to diverse perspectives, cultures, and experiences, broadening their understanding of the world and challenging their preconceived notions. Similarly, knowledge acquisition can lead to cognitive awakening by expanding one's intellectual capacity, encouraging critical thinking, and fostering a curiosity-driven mindset. It is important to note that while wealth and knowledge can facilitate cognitive awakening, they are not guarantees of it. Cognitive awakening is a deeply personal and subjective process that involves introspection, self-reflection, and a willingness to question and challenge one's beliefs and assumptions. It can occur regardless of one's financial status or educational background. In conclusion, the relationship between wealth, knowledge, and cognitive awakening is intricate and interdependent. Wealth can provide access to knowledge, while knowledge can contribute to wealth creation. Both wealth and knowledge can also play a role in fostering cognitive awakening by exposing individuals to new ideas, broadening their perspectives, and encouraging personal development.

The intricate relationship of wealth, knowledge, and cognitive awakening is an interesting topic to explore. Wealth can provide individuals with access to better education and resources, which in turn can enhance their knowledge. This acquisition of knowledge can have a profound impact on cognitive awakening, expanding one's intellectual capabilities and understanding of the world. Conversely, cognitive awakening can also lead to the accumulation of wealth, as individuals employ their enhanced cognitive abilities to pursue opportunities, make informed decisions, and create value. However, it's important to note that wealth and knowledge are not always directly correlated, and cognitive awakening can occur regardless of one's socioeconomic status. Ultimately, the interplay between wealth, knowledge, and cognitive awakening is complex and multifaceted, deserving of further exploration and study.

CHAPTER 2
NEW METHODS FOR CONDUCTING BUSINESS WITH A.I. AND CHATGPT

Artificial Intelligence (AI) and ChatGPT have revolutionized the way businesses operate and interact with customers. Here are some new methods for conducting business with AI and ChatGPT:

1. Virtual Assistants: AI-powered virtual assistants can handle customer inquiries, provide support, and assist with various tasks. These assistants can be integrated into websites, mobile apps, or messaging platforms, allowing businesses to provide 24/7 customer service without human intervention. Virtual assistants can handle routine queries, provide product recommendations, and even process transactions.

2. Personalized Customer Experiences: AI algorithms can analyze vast amounts of customer data to understand individual preferences, behaviors, and purchase history. This information can be used to create personalized recommendations, offers, and marketing campaigns. By leveraging AI, businesses can tailor their interactions with customers, enhancing customer satisfaction and loyalty.

3. Chatbots for Sales and Lead Generation: Chatbots powered by AI can engage with potential customers, answer their questions, and guide them through the sales process. These chatbots can qualify leads, provide product information, and even make personalized recommendations based on customer preferences. By automating parts of the sales process, businesses can increase efficiency and improve conversion rates.

4. Data Analysis and Insights: AI algorithms can analyze large datasets to uncover patterns, trends, and insights that can inform business strategies. By leveraging AI for data analysis, businesses can gain a deeper understanding of customer behavior, market trends, and competitive landscapes. This information can be used to make data-driven decisions, optimize operations, and identify new business opportunities.

5. Natural Language Processing (NLP) for Customer Support: ChatGPT and other NLP models can understand and respond to customer queries in a conversational manner. By training these models on vast amounts of customer support data, businesses can automate responses to common customer inquiries, reducing the workload on human support agents. NLP models can also be used to analyze customer sentiment, identify issues, and improve overall customer support experiences.

6. AI-Powered Content Generation: AI can assist in generating content for marketing purposes. ChatGPT and similar models can be trained on existing content to generate blog posts, social media captions, product descriptions, and more. This can save time and resources for businesses while maintaining a consistent brand voice.

7. Predictive Analytics: AI algorithms can analyze historical data to make predictions about future trends, customer behavior, and market dynamics. By leveraging predictive analytics, businesses can optimize inventory management, anticipate customer needs, and make proactive business decisions. It is important to note that while AI and ChatGPT offer numerous benefits, human oversight and intervention are still crucial. Businesses should ensure that AI systems are regularly monitored, updated, and refined to maintain accuracy and relevance. Additionally, ethical considerations, data privacy, and transparency should be prioritized when implementing AI solutions in business operations.

CHAPTER 2
TRANSITION FROM CYBER ECONOMY TO A.I. + CHATGPT ECONOMY

The transition from the cyber economy to an AI and ChatGPT economy represents an evolution in the way we interact with and utilize technology. The cyber economy, also known as the digital economy, refers to the economic activities and transactions that take place online. It encompasses a wide range of industries, including e-commerce, digital services, and online platforms.

With the advancement of artificial intelligence (AI) and the development of language models like ChatGPT, we are witnessing a shift in how technology interacts with humans. AI has the potential to automate various tasks, augment human capabilities, and provide personalized experiences. ChatGPT, specifically, is a language model designed to generate human-like text responses, enabling conversational interactions.

In an AI and ChatGPT economy, we can expect to see several changes:

Automation and Efficiency: AI technologies can automate routine tasks, leading to increased efficiency and productivity. This can free up human workers to focus on more complex and creative endeavors.

Personalized Experiences: AI algorithms can analyze vast amounts of data to better understand individual preferences and tailor experiences accordingly. This can enhance customer satisfaction and drive personalized marketing approaches.

New Business Models: The AI economy may give rise to new business models and revenue streams. Companies can leverage AI capabilities to offer innovative services, such as virtual assistants, personalized recommendations, and predictive analytics.

Ethical Considerations: As AI becomes more prevalent, it raises ethical concerns related to data privacy, algorithmic bias, and the impact on employment. Regulations and guidelines will need to be developed to address these challenges and ensure responsible AI usage.

Skill Requirements: The shift to an AI and ChatGPT economy will require individuals to acquire new skills. There will be a growing demand for professionals with expertise in AI development, data analysis, and human-machine interaction.

It's important to note that the transition to an AI and ChatGPT economy is a gradual process that will unfold over time. While AI technologies hold immense potential, their deployment and integration into various industries will require careful consideration of social, economic, and ethical implications.

CHAPTER 4
NEW ECONOMY, NEW SCIENTIFIC BREAKTHROUGHS, NEW SOCIAL CHANGES, NEW POLITICAL CHANGES AND NEW ECONOMY

The idea of the M. R. M. Millennium Renaissance Movement can indeed encompass various aspects, including new economy, scientific breakthroughs, social changes, political changes, and economic transformations. Let's explore each of these elements within the context of a potential M. R. M.

New Economy: The M. R. M. can be marked by the emergence of new economic models or paradigms. This could involve the rise of innovative industries, disruptive technologies, and novel approaches to commerce and trade. For example, the Renaissance in Europe saw the transition from feudalism to a more market-oriented economy, with the growth of mercantilism and the establishment of capitalist systems.

Scientific Breakthroughs: The M. R. M. will witness significant advancements in scientific knowledge and understanding. These breakthroughs can lead to revolutionary discoveries, transformative inventions, and paradigm shifts in various scientific disciplines. The old Renaissance period itself was characterized by groundbreaking developments in fields like astronomy, physics, anatomy, and mathematics, with figures like Copernicus, Galileo, and Leonardo da Vinci making notable contributions.

Social Changes: The M. R. M. can bring about profound social transformations, challenging existing norms and fostering new social structures. This could involve shifts in societal values, attitudes, and cultural practices. The Renaissance in Europe, for instance, saw the emergence of humanism, a renewed focus on individualism, and a reevaluation of traditional religious beliefs.

Political Changes: The M. R. M. can be accompanied by significant political changes, including shifts in power dynamics, governance systems, and ideologies. It may involve the rise of new political movements, the establishment of new forms of government, or the reformation of existing political institutions. The old Renaissance witnessed the rise of city-states, the spread of republicanism, and the questioning of absolute monarchies.

New ChatGPT Economy: A brand new economy will be the core aspect of a M. R.M., as mentioned earlier. It involves not just economic models but also novel approaches to wealth creation, distribution, and resource management. The old Renaissance period witnessed the growth of trade, the expansion of banking systems, and the development of new economic philosophies that laid the foundation for modern capitalism.

In summary, the M. R. M. Millennium Renaissance Movement will encompasses a multidimensional transformation that can manifest in various aspects of society, including the economy, science, social structures, politics, and more. It is a time of great intellectual, cultural, and societal flourishing, often driven by visionary individuals and a collective desire for progress and renewal.

CHAPTER 5
101 METHODS FOR MAKING MONEY FOR THE INDIVIDUALS WITH CHATGPT

1. Offering personalized writing services, such as creating blog posts, articles, or social media content.
2. Providing proofreading and editing services for written content.
3. Offering virtual assistant services, such as managing emails, scheduling appointments, or conducting research.
4. Providing language translation services for individuals or businesses.
5. Offering resume writing and cover letter services.
6. Providing online tutoring or educational assistance in various subjects.
7. Offering personalized career coaching and guidance.
8. Providing personalized financial planning advice and budgeting assistance.
9. Offering personalized fitness and nutrition coaching.
10. Providing personalized relationship advice and counseling.
11. Offering personalized travel planning services, including itinerary creation and recommendations.
12. Providing personalized fashion styling and wardrobe consulting.
13. Offering personalized home organization and decluttering advice.
14. Providing personalized interior design recommendations and tips.
15. Offering personalized gardening and landscaping advice.
16. Providing personalized pet care and training tips.
17. Offering personalized DIY project ideas and instructions.
18. Providing personalized health and wellness advice.
19. Offering personalized technology and gadget recommendations.
20. Providing personalized music recommendations and playlist creation.
21. Offering personalized book recommendations and reading lists.
22. Providing personalized art and creative inspiration.
23. Offering personalized mindfulness and meditation guidance.
24. Providing personalized productivity and time management tips.

25. Offering personalized language learning assistance and practice.
26. Providing personalized cooking and recipe suggestions.
27. Offering personalized financial investment advice.
28. Providing personalized parenting tips and advice.
29. Offering personalized event planning and organization assistance.
30. Providing personalized home repair and maintenance advice.
31. Offering personalized photography tips and techniques.
32. Providing personalized business and entrepreneurship advice.
33. Offering personalized marketing and branding strategies.
34. Providing personalized social media management and growth strategies.
35. Offering personalized graphic design and visual content creation.
36. Providing personalized video editing and post-production services.
37. Offering personalized website design and development services.
38. Providing personalized software and app recommendations.
39. Offering personalized coding and programming assistance.
40. Providing personalized data analysis and insights.
41. Offering personalized legal advice and consultation.
42. Providing personalized real estate and property investment advice.
43. Offering personalized automotive tips and maintenance advice.
44. Providing personalized travel photography tips and techniques.
45. Offering personalized event photography services.
46. Providing personalized wedding planning and coordination assistance.
47. Offering personalized party planning and decoration ideas.
48. Providing personalized social media advertising strategies.
49. Offering personalized content marketing and SEO advice.
50. Providing personalized influencer marketing strategies.
51. Offering personalized customer service and support.
52. Providing personalized market research and analysis.
53. Offering personalized project management and organization.
54. Providing personalized data entry and administrative support.
55. Offering personalized transcription services for audio or video content.
56. Providing personalized voice-over services for videos or commercials.

57. Offering personalized virtual reality (VR) experience recommendations.
58. Providing personalized augmented reality (AR) app suggestions.
59. Offering personalized cryptocurrency investment advice.
60. Providing personalized cybersecurity tips and recommendations.
61. Offering personalized ethical hacking and vulnerability testing.
62. Providing personalized drone photography and videography services.
63. Offering personalized 3D modeling and design services.
64. Providing personalized virtual tour creation for real estate or tourism.
65. Offering personalized language interpretation services for conferences or events.
66. Providing personalized music production and composition services.
67. Offering personalized podcast editing and production services.
68. Providing personalized voice acting and narration services.
69. Offering personalized AI chatbot development and implementation.
70. Providing personalized virtual reality (VR) game development services.
71. Offering personalized augmented reality (AR) app development services.
72. Providing personalized website or app testing and quality assurance.
73. Offering personalized data visualization and infographic design.
74. Providing personalized drone piloting and aerial photography services.
75. Offering personalized video game testing and bug reporting.
76. Providing personalized virtual reality (VR) training and simulation development.
77. Offering personalized augmented reality (AR) marketing campaigns.
78. Providing personalized AI-powered customer support chatbot development.

79. Offering personalized virtual reality (VR) therapy and relaxation experiences.
80. Providing personalized augmented reality (AR) educational content development.
81. Offering personalized AI-powered personal assistant app development.
82. Providing personalized virtual reality (VR) fitness and exercise programs.
83. Offering personalized augmented reality (AR) fashion and beauty experiences.
84. Providing personalized AI-powered language learning apps and platforms.
85. Offering personalized virtual reality (VR) architectural visualization services.
86. Providing personalized augmented reality (AR) museum and exhibition experiences.
87. Offering personalized AI-powered financial planning and investment apps.
88. Providing personalized virtual reality (VR) travel and exploration experiences.
89. Offering personalized augmented reality (AR) gaming and entertainment apps.
90. Providing personalized AI-powered healthcare and medical diagnosis apps.
91. Offering personalized virtual reality (VR) art and creative experiences.
92. Providing personalized augmented reality
93. Offering personalized AI-powered language translation apps and services.
94. Providing personalized virtual reality (VR) sports and training simulations.
95. Offering personalized augmented reality (AR) shopping and retail experiences.
96. Providing personalized AI-powered productivity and task management apps.

97. Offering personalized virtual reality (VR) educational and learning experiences.
98. Providing personalized augmented reality (AR) navigation and mapping apps.
99. Offering personalized AI-powered personal finance and budgeting apps.
100. Providing personalized virtual reality (VR) storytelling and narrative experiences.
101. Offering personalized augmented reality (AR) social media and networking apps.

PART 3
INFLUENCE OF A.I. AND COGNITIVE AWAKENING ON OUR NEW TECHNOLOGIES

CHAPTER I
BIOTECHNOLOGY + GENETIC ENGINEERING

Artificial intelligence (AI) has had a significant impact on biotechnology and genetic engineering, revolutionizing the field in numerous ways. Here are some of the key influences of AI in these areas:

1. Data analysis and processing: Biotechnology and genetic engineering generate massive amounts of data, such as DNA sequences, genomic profiles, and protein structures. AI algorithms are used to analyze, interpret, and make sense of this information, enabling researchers to identify patterns, detect mutations, and make predictions. AI-driven tools have greatly accelerated the process of data analysis, allowing researchers to gain insights more quickly and effectively.

2. Drug discovery and development: AI is transforming the process of drug discovery by enabling more efficient identification of potential drug candidates. Machine learning algorithms can analyze biological data, molecular structures, and pharmacological properties to predict compounds that are likely to have specific therapeutic effects. This helps in streamlining the discovery and development of new drugs, reducing the time and cost involved.

3. Precision medicine: AI is enhancing the field of precision medicine, which focuses on tailoring medical treatments to an individual's genetic profile. With AI, genetic data can be efficiently analyzed and personalized treatment plans can be developed based on an individual's unique genetic makeup, lifestyle, and medical history. AI algorithms can also assist in predicting disease outcomes and potential side effects, leading to more targeted and effective interventions.

4. Gene editing and CRISPR technology: AI is being employed to improve the efficiency and accuracy of gene editing techniques,

particularly CRISPR-Cas9. Machine learning algorithms help in designing highly specific guide RNAs for targeting specific genetic sequences, improving the precision and success of gene editing procedures. This advancement has potential implications across various areas, including agriculture, therapeutics, and bioengineering.

5. Automation and robotics: AI-driven automation and robotics have transformed laboratory processes in biotechnology and genetic engineering. Robotic systems, guided by AI algorithms, can handle routine laboratory tasks, such as sample preparation, DNA sequencing, and high-throughput screening, with enhanced precision, speed, and efficiency. This enables researchers to focus on more complex and creative aspects of their work.

6. Ethical considerations: AI also plays a role in addressing ethical challenges in biotechnology. It can assist in analyzing and managing ethical issues related to genetic engineering, such as identifying potential risks and considering societal implications. AI can support ethical decision-making processes and ensure responsible practices are followed.

Overall, AI has had a profound influence on biotechnology and genetic engineering, revolutionizing data analysis, drug discovery, precision medicine, gene editing, laboratory automation, and ethical considerations. Its continued integration holds great promise for advancing these fields and unlocking new possibilities in understanding, manipulating, and exploiting biological systems.

CHAPTER 2
NANOTECHNOLOGY

Artificial intelligence (AI) has a significant influence on nanotechnology, contributing to advancements in various aspects of this field. Here are some of the key influences of AI on nanotechnology:

1. Materials discovery and design: Nanotechnology involves the manipulation and engineering of materials at the nanoscale. AI algorithms, such as machine learning and data mining, can facilitate the discovery and design of new nanomaterials with desired properties. By analyzing large datasets and correlations between material properties, AI can assist in predicting and identifying new materials that exhibit specific characteristics, leading to more efficient and targeted material synthesis.

2. Nanostructure prediction and modeling: AI techniques, including molecular dynamics simulations and quantum mechanics calculations, can help predict and model the behavior and properties of nanostructures. These simulations can provide valuable insights into the interactions and properties of nanoscale materials, aiding in the design of more effective and efficient nanodevices and nanosystems.

3. Nanofabrication and manufacturing: AI can play a vital role in optimizing nanofabrication processes and improving manufacturing efficiency in nanotechnology. Machine learning algorithms can analyze and interpret data from nanofabrication tools, enabling real-time process monitoring, quality control, and automation. This optimizes manufacturing processes, reduces defects, and enhances the reproducibility of nanoscale devices and structures.

4. Nanoscale imaging and characterization: AI algorithms can enhance the capabilities of nanoscale imaging and characterization techniques. By leveraging machine learning, image recognition, and pattern analysis, AI can assist in the interpretation and analysis of complex nanoscale

images and data. This helps researchers extract more meaningful information from images, gain deeper insights into nanoscale phenomena, and improve the accuracy of characterization techniques.

5. Nano-enhanced AI systems: Nanostructures and nanomaterials can be integrated into AI systems to enhance their performance. For example, nanoscale sensors and devices can be utilized to improve data collection and sensing capabilities, leading to more accurate and sensitive AI systems. Nanomaterials can also be incorporated into AI hardware, such as neuromorphic computing, to enhance computing power and energy efficiency.

6. Nanomedicine and drug delivery: AI techniques can be applied to nanomedicine and drug delivery systems. AI algorithms can aid in the design and optimization of nanocarriers for targeted drug delivery, allowing for personalized medicine approaches. Additionally, AI can contribute to the modeling and prediction of nanoparticle behavior within biological systems, aiding in the development of more effective therapeutic strategies.

Overall, AI brings significant advancements and opportunities to various aspects of nanotechnology, including materials discovery, nanostructure prediction, fabrication, imaging, and the integration of nanomaterials into AI systems. These synergistic interactions between AI and nanotechnology have the potential to drive innovation and impact multiple sectors, from electronics and energy to medicine and environmental applications.

CHAPTER 3
HIGH END SEMI CONDUCTOR CHIPS

Artificial intelligence (AI) has a substantial influence on the development and production of high-end semiconductor chips. Here are some key influences of AI on this domain:

1. Chip design and optimization: AI plays a crucial role in chip design and optimization. Designing high-performance and power-efficient chips involves complex trade-offs and parameter tuning. AI algorithms, such as genetic algorithms or reinforcement learning, can help automate and expedite the design process by exploring a vast design space and finding optimal solutions. This leads to more efficient chip architectures, improved performance, and reduced power consumption.

2. Manufacturing process enhancement: AI enhances the manufacturing process of high-end semiconductor chips. AI techniques like machine learning and data analytics can analyze large volumes of sensor data collected during chip manufacturing, enabling real-time decision-making and process optimization. This helps identify and address manufacturing defects, improve yield rates, and enhance overall chip quality.

3. Quality assurance and testing: AI plays a crucial role in quality assurance and testing of high-end semiconductor chips. Machine learning algorithms can analyze test results and identify patterns or anomalies, which helps in fault detection, diagnosis, and root cause analysis. This speeds up the testing process, improves reliability, and reduces costly rework.

4. Predictive maintenance: AI algorithms can enable predictive maintenance for semiconductor chip manufacturing equipment. By analyzing sensor data, AI can identify early signs of equipment degradation or failure, allowing for timely maintenance. This prevents

unexpected downtime, optimizes equipment utilization, and reduces costs associated with unscheduled repairs.

5. AI accelerators and specialized chip architectures: The demand for AI applications has led to the development of specialized chip architectures designed for AI workloads. These AI accelerators, like graphics processing units (GPUs) or tensor processing units (TPUs), incorporate AI-focused design principles to efficiently perform AI computations. They enable the acceleration of AI algorithms and significantly enhance the performance of AI applications.

6. Quantum computing: While still in its early stages, AI is influencing the development of high-end semiconductor chips for quantum computing. Quantum computers have the potential to solve complex AI problems more efficiently. Semiconductor chip manufacturers are exploring the integration of quantum computing technologies with traditional chip architectures to unlock new capabilities and advance AI research.

Overall, AI has had a significant impact on high-end semiconductor chips, shaping the chip design process, optimizing manufacturing, improving quality assurance and testing, enabling predictive maintenance, driving the development of specialized AI accelerators, and opening new possibilities in quantum computing. AI continues to drive innovation in this domain, contributing to advancements in performance, efficiency, and functionality of high-end semiconductor chips.

CHAPTER 4
VIRTUAL REALITY, AUGMENTED REALITY

Artificial intelligence (AI) has a significant influence on the development and application of both virtual reality (VR) and augmented reality (AR) technologies. Here are some key influences of AI in these domains:

1. Real-time tracking and object recognition: AI algorithms play a crucial role in real-time tracking and object recognition within VR and AR experiences. By leveraging computer vision techniques and deep learning algorithms, AI can identify and track objects, gestures, and facial expressions in real-time. This enables immersive and interactive experiences where virtual elements are seamlessly integrated with the user's environment.

2. Natural language processing and voice recognition: AI-powered natural language processing and voice recognition technologies enhance VR and AR experiences. This allows users to interact with virtual objects and characters using voice commands, leading to more intuitive and immersive experiences. AI algorithms enable speech recognition and understanding, enabling more natural and responsive interactions in VR and AR environments.

3. Personalization and adaptive experiences: AI enables personalized and adaptive experiences in VR and AR. By leveraging machine learning algorithms and user data, AI can understand user preferences, habits, and behavior patterns. This allows VR and AR systems to adapt content, visuals, and interactions to each user's preferences, creating more engaging and tailored experiences.

4. Content generation and recommendation: AI can automate and enhance content generation for VR and AR applications. AI algorithms can analyze vast amounts of user data, such as browsing history and preferences, to generate personalized content recommendations. Additionally, AI can automate the creation of virtual environments,

characters, and objects, reducing the time and effort required to develop immersive VR and AR experiences.

5. Realistic simulations and intelligent agents: AI enables the creation of intelligent agents and realistic simulations within VR and AR. By incorporating AI algorithms, virtual characters and agents can exhibit more natural and intelligent behavior, responding dynamically to user interactions. This enhances the realism and immersion of VR and AR experiences, making them more lifelike and interactive.

6. Data analytics and insights: AI techniques facilitate data analytics within VR and AR environments. AI algorithms can analyze user interactions, navigation patterns, and engagement metrics to extract insights and generate actionable information. This helps developers and content creators optimize experiences, make informed design decisions, and improve the overall user experience.

Overall, AI has a profound influence on VR and AR, driving advancements in real-time tracking, natural language processing, personalization, content generation, intelligent agents, data analytics, and more. By integrating AI capabilities, VR and AR technologies become more immersive, interactive, and tailored to individual users, enhancing their overall value and potential applications in various industries.

CHAPTER 5
MACHINE LEARNING

Artificial intelligence (AI) and machine learning (ML) have a highly interconnected relationship, as AI techniques often rely on ML algorithms to learn from data and make intelligent decisions. Here are some key ways in which AI influences machine learning:

1. Algorithm development and advancement: AI research and development contribute to the advancement and development of new ML algorithms. AI techniques such as deep learning, reinforcement learning, and generative models have propelled significant progress in ML. These advanced algorithms enable more complex and accurate predictions, classifications, and decision-making, expanding the capabilities of ML systems.

2. Automation and efficiency: AI plays a key role in automating and optimizing various aspects of ML processes. AI algorithms, such as genetic algorithms or Bayesian optimization, assist in hyperparameter tuning and model selection, enabling automated optimization of ML models. Additionally, AI techniques facilitate automated feature engineering by identifying relevant features from raw data, saving time and effort for practitioners.

3. Scalability and big data processing: AI technologies contribute to the scalability of ML models and the processing of big data. AI algorithms help in handling and processing large volumes of data by employing parallel computing, distributed systems, and cloud computing. This allows ML models to process and learn from massive datasets efficiently, unlocking insights and patterns that would be challenging to discover using traditional methods.

4. Transfer learning and knowledge sharing: AI techniques enable transfer learning, where knowledge acquired from one ML task is applied to another related task. Transfer learning helps in solving new problems

with limited data by leveraging pre-trained models and knowledge gained from previous tasks. This ability to transfer knowledge accelerates the learning process, enhances generalization, and reduces the need for extensive data collection for each new task.

5. Model interpretability and explainability: AI techniques contribute to enhancing the interpretability and explainability of ML models. Interpretable AI methods, such as decision trees or rule-based systems, enable ML models to provide understandable explanations and justifications for their predictions or decisions. This is particularly useful in domains where transparency and accountability are crucial.

6. Reinforcement learning and autonomous systems: AI influences ML through reinforcement learning, which involves training agents to interact with an environment and learn from feedback to maximize rewards. Reinforcement learning enables the development of autonomous systems that can make decisions and take actions in complex environments. This has applications in robotics, autonomous vehicles, and other areas where adaptive decision-making is required.

Overall, AI has a significant influence on the field of machine learning, driving algorithm development, automation, scalability, transfer learning, interpretability, and the emergence of autonomous systems. As AI continues to evolve, it will likely further shape and advance the capabilities of machine learning, leading to more intelligent, efficient, and impactful applications across various industries.

Brave New World of A.I. & A.I.
Artificial Intelligence & Anthropoid Intelligence

CHAPTER 6
QUANTUM COMPUTING

Artificial intelligence (AI) has the potential to significantly influence the field of quantum computing, as it can facilitate advancements in problem-solving, optimization, and data analysis. Here are some ways in which AI influences quantum computing:

1. Quantum machine learning: AI can facilitate the development of quantum machine learning algorithms. Quantum machine learning combines the power of both quantum computing and AI techniques to tackle complex tasks. AI algorithms can help in training and optimizing quantum machine learning models, enabling more efficient and accurate predictions, classifications, and decision-making in quantum computing.

2. Quantum optimization: AI techniques can be applied to optimize and improve the performance of quantum algorithms. Quantum optimization problems, which involve finding the optimal solution from a large set of possibilities, can benefit from AI algorithms, such as genetic algorithms or reinforcement learning, to search for better solutions. AI can assist in optimizing quantum circuits, quantum error correction, and other aspects of quantum computing.

3. Quantum data analysis: AI can enhance the analysis of data generated from quantum experiments or quantum simulations. By leveraging AI algorithms, such as pattern recognition or clustering, quantum data can be processed and interpreted more effectively, leading to valuable insights or discoveries in areas like quantum chemistry, material science, or optimization problems.

4. Quantum control and error correction: AI can contribute to the development of intelligent control and error correction techniques in quantum systems. AI algorithms can learn and adapt to quantum noise and errors, enabling more efficient error correction and fault tolerance.

These techniques are essential in ensuring the reliability and stability of quantum computers in practice.

5. Quantum neural networks: AI and quantum computing can work together to develop quantum neural networks (QNN). QNNs are networks designed to process and interpret quantum data, enabling the application of AI techniques in quantum information processing, pattern recognition, and optimization problems. QNNs have the potential to leverage the capabilities of both AI and quantum computing for more sophisticated problem-solving.

6. Quantum-inspired algorithms: AI can draw inspiration from quantum computing principles to develop innovative algorithms. Quantum-inspired algorithms, known as classical algorithms inspired by quantum concepts, can exploit quantum properties to solve certain complex problems more efficiently than classical algorithms alone. These algorithms bridge the gap between AI and quantum computing, offering the potential for improved performance and efficiency in specific applications.

Overall, AI has the potential to push the boundaries of quantum computing by providing optimization, data analysis, error correction, control, and novel algorithmic approaches. The synergy between AI and quantum computing could lead to breakthroughs in solving complex problems and unlocking the full potential of quantum technologies for numerous applications.

CHAPTER 7
SPACE PROPULSION TECHNOLOGY

Artificial intelligence (AI) has the potential to greatly influence space propulsion technology, enhancing efficiency, safety, and decision-making processes. Here are some ways in which AI influences space propulsion technology:

1. Autonomous spacecraft control: AI can enable autonomous control systems for spacecraft propulsion. AI algorithms can analyze sensor data and make real-time decisions to optimize propulsion systems, adjust trajectory, and manage fuel consumption. This autonomy reduces the need for constant human intervention and enables more efficient and responsive spacecraft operations.

2. Propulsion system optimization: AI techniques can be employed to optimize the design and performance of space propulsion systems. By leveraging AI algorithms, such as genetic algorithms or reinforcement learning, engineers can search for the best configuration, materials, or parameters for propulsion engines, leading to improved efficiency, thrust, and reliability.

3. Fault detection and diagnosis: AI can assist in detecting and diagnosing faults in propulsion systems. Machine learning algorithms can analyze sensor data and identify anomalies or patterns associated with potential failures or malfunctions. This early detection allows for timely repairs or adjustments, ensuring the safe operation of propulsion systems during space missions.

4. Trajectory optimization and navigation: AI algorithms can optimize spacecraft trajectories and navigation in complex space environments. By considering various factors such as gravity assists, orbital dynamics, and mission objectives, AI can calculate optimal trajectories that minimize fuel consumption or reduce travel time. This improves mission efficiency and enables more precise navigation in space.

5. Predictive maintenance: AI techniques can facilitate predictive maintenance for propulsion systems. By analyzing operational data and performance trends, AI algorithms can predict potential failures or degradation in advance. This allows for proactive maintenance scheduling and reduces the risk of unexpected system failures during critical missions.

6. Data analysis and anomaly detection: AI algorithms can analyze large volumes of data collected from space missions to identify patterns, anomalies, or potential discoveries related to propulsion technology. AI can aid in analyzing propulsion performance data, fuel efficiency, and other parameters, assisting scientists and engineers in improving propulsion systems or discovering new phenomena.

7. Simulation and optimization of new propulsion concepts: AI can accelerate the simulation and optimization processes for novel propulsion concepts. By leveraging AI algorithms, researchers can quickly iterate through various designs, test scenarios, and parameters to identify promising solutions. This expedites the development of new propulsion technologies and enables faster innovation in the field.

Overall, AI has the potential to revolutionize space propulsion technology by enabling autonomous control, optimizing propulsion systems, detecting faults, optimizing trajectories, facilitating predictive maintenance, analyzing data, and accelerating the development of innovative propulsion concepts. These advancements contribute to safer, more efficient, and more capable space missions in the future.

CHAPTER 8
WORMHOLE TECHNOLOGIES

It's important to note that wormholes, as hypothetical structures that could potentially connect distant points in spacetime, are still theoretical and have not been observed or proven to exist. However, if wormhole technology were to be developed in the future, artificial intelligence (AI) could potentially have several influences on its study, understanding, and practical implementation:

1. Data analysis and modeling: AI algorithms could help analyze and interpret vast amounts of data from cosmological observations and simulations related to wormholes. AI-powered data analysis techniques could identify patterns, correlations, and potential signatures of wormholes in complex datasets, assisting scientists in refining theoretical models.

2. Design and optimization: AI algorithms could aid in optimizing the structure and properties of potential wormholes. By employing machine learning algorithms, scientists could develop optimization techniques to find the most efficient and stable configurations for sustaining the wormhole's structure and manipulating its gravitational properties.

3. Quantum computing support: As quantum computing technologies advance, AI can complement their capabilities by developing specialized algorithms for modeling and simulating wormholes. Quantum-inspired algorithms running on quantum computers can potentially tackle complex calculations required for understanding the behavior and properties of wormholes.

4. Simulation and visualization: AI-powered simulation techniques can aid in recreating and visualizing the behavior and effects of wormholes. By simulating interactions of matter, energy, and spacetime around wormholes, scientists can better understand and study the potential implications for space travel and time dilation.

5. Navigation and control: AI could be relevant in future scenarios where wormholes are used for interstellar travel. AI algorithms could assist in navigating spaceships through wormholes, optimizing trajectories, and adjusting propulsion systems to ensure safe and efficient travel, while accounting for relativistic effects and potential fluctuations in spacetime.

6. Security and stability: AI could play a role in monitoring and maintaining the stability and security of wormhole structures. By continuously analyzing sensor data and evaluating the structural integrity of the wormhole, AI systems could detect and respond to potential threats or instabilities, ensuring the safe passage of objects or spacecraft.

It's important to emphasize that the study and practical implementation of wormholes remain purely speculative at this point. While AI may have potential applications in various aspects, the development and realization of wormhole technologies are still primarily within the realm of theoretical physics and speculative science fiction.

PART 4:
INFLUENCE OF A.I. AND COGNITIVE AWAKENING ON SOCIETY

CHAPTER 1
WILL A.I. MAKE THE RICH RICHER AND THOSE IN POWER MORE POWERFUL?

The impact of AI on wealth distribution and power dynamics is a complex topic without a definitive answer. While AI has the potential to contribute to economic growth and innovation, its effects on wealth distribution can be influenced by various factors, including societal decisions, regulations, and ethical considerations. Here are a few factors to consider:

1. Automation and job displacement: AI-driven automation has the potential to impact employment across various industries. This can lead to job displacement, particularly in areas dominated by routine and repetitive tasks. If not managed properly, there is a possibility that the rich and those in power could benefit from increased productivity and profits, while workers in certain sectors might face job insecurity. However, this impact can be mitigated through strategies like retraining programs, transitioning to new industries, and equitable distribution of the benefits derived from AI technologies.

2. Skill requirements: The rise of AI may create demand for new skills and expertise. Those who can adapt and acquire the necessary skills to work with AI technologies may have better employment opportunities and potentially higher incomes. However, ensuring widespread access to education and training is crucial to prevent a growing divide between those who can afford to acquire these skills and those who can't.

3. Access to AI systems and data: AI systems rely on large amounts of data for training and operation. Access to quality data and robust computing resources can be a significant determinant of AI success. Entities that have access to vast amounts of data and resources, such as large corporations or governments, may have an advantage in utilizing AI effectively. Ensuring data privacy, promoting open data initiatives, and implementing regulations on data monopolies can help foster a more inclusive and competitive AI landscape.

4. Bias and fairness: AI systems are only as unbiased as the data they are trained on and the algorithms used. If biases are not addressed and diversity is not considered during the development of AI systems, there is a risk that AI can reinforce existing inequalities or discriminate against certain groups. Efforts to promote fairness, transparency, and ethical standards in AI development can aid in mitigating these risks and ensuring more equitable outcomes.

It is important for policymakers, organizations, and society as a whole to actively address these challenges and ensure that AI technologies are developed and deployed with a focus on fairness, inclusivity, and equal access. By considering the potential societal implications and making informed decisions, it is possible to shape AI in a way that benefits a broader range of people rather than solely benefiting the rich and powerful.

CHAPTER 2
WILL A.I. SOLVE OUR SOCIAL ILLS, SUCH AS CRIME, OVER POPULATION, ENVIRONMENT AND POVERTY?

AI has the potential to contribute positively in addressing some social challenges, but it is important to understand that it is not a panacea that can single-handedly solve all complex societal problems. Here's a closer look at how AI could play a role in tackling these issues:

1. Crime: AI can be utilized in various ways to enhance crime prevention and law enforcement. For instance, predictive analytics and machine learning algorithms can help identify patterns and analyze vast amounts of data to anticipate criminal activity, enabling authorities to allocate resources more effectively. AI-enabled surveillance systems can assist in real-time monitoring and threat detection. However, ethical considerations such as privacy, bias, and potential misuse must be carefully managed to ensure a fair and just implementation.

2. Overpopulation: While AI cannot directly address overpopulation, it can contribute indirectly to managing its consequences. AI technologies can assist in urban planning, transportation optimization, and resource allocation, leading to more efficient utilization of infrastructure and better management of resources in densely populated areas. AI-powered simulations and predictive models can help policymakers make informed decisions regarding population growth and its impact on various sectors.

3. Environment: AI can aid in environmental conservation efforts. Machine learning algorithms can analyze large environmental datasets, such as satellite imagery, to detect patterns and identify areas at risk or impacted by climate change. AI can also help optimize energy

consumption, improve waste management systems, and enhance environmental monitoring and conservation efforts.

4. Poverty: AI has the potential to contribute to poverty alleviation through various means. Access to AI-driven educational platforms and online learning can help democratize education and provide skills training to underserved populations. AI-powered tools and platforms can facilitate better financial inclusion, access to healthcare and other vital services in underprivileged areas. However, addressing poverty involves multifaceted approaches encompassing economic policies, social programs, and systemic changes, where AI is just one contributing factor.

It is worth noting that the ethical implications of AI applications need continual consideration. Issues like bias, fairness, privacy, and transparency must be addressed to ensure that AI technologies don't inadvertently exacerbate existing social inequities and vulnerabilities.

Ultimately, solving complex social and global challenges requires not only technological advancements but also interdisciplinary collaboration, policy changes, and collective societal efforts. AI can be a valuable tool, but it must be combined with a holistic approach that includes social, political, and economic considerations to create meaningful and sustainable solutions.

CHAPTER 3
WILL A.I. HELP THE INDIVIDUALS TOWARDS GREATER EMPOWERMENT AND SATISFACTION.

Yes, AI has the potential to empower individuals and enhance overall satisfaction in various ways :

1. Personalization: AI technologies can analyze vast amounts of data about individuals' preferences, behaviors, and needs, enabling personalized experiences. From personalized recommendations in entertainment and shopping to personalized healthcare and education, AI can tailor services and offerings to meet individual requirements, leading to greater satisfaction.

2. Productivity and Efficiency: AI can automate routine and repetitive tasks, freeing up time for individuals to focus on more meaningful and creative endeavors. AI-powered tools and platforms can assist in managing schedules, organizing tasks, and providing real-time assistance, thereby improving productivity and empowering individuals to achieve their goals more effectively.

3. Information Access: AI-powered search engines and virtual assistants can provide instant access to information, enabling individuals to find answers and resources quickly and easily. This can empower individuals to make more informed decisions, stay updated on current events, and acquire knowledge in various domains, ultimately leading to personal growth and satisfaction.

4. Assistive Technology: AI can assist individuals with disabilities or special needs through the development of assistive technologies. These technologies, ranging from voice-controlled assistants to mobility aids, can enhance independence, accessibility, and overall quality of life for individuals with diverse abilities.

5. Healthcare Advancements: AI technologies can contribute to advancements in healthcare, including personalized medicine, early disease detection, and improved diagnostics. By providing more accurate diagnoses, suggesting tailored treatment plans, and empowering individuals with health-related insights, AI can enhance overall well-being and satisfaction.

6. Communication and Social Interaction: AI-powered chatbots and virtual assistants can facilitate efficient and user-friendly communication platforms. This can enhance social interactions, offer support, and improve accessibility for individuals, including those who may face barriers in traditional forms of communication.

However, it's crucial to strike a balance between the potential benefits of AI and considering potential risks and challenges. Ethical considerations, transparency, privacy, and the human-centric design of AI systems are essential to ensure that AI serves the best interests of individuals and respects their autonomy.

Overall, while AI holds promise in empowering individuals and contributing to greater satisfaction, it needs to be thoughtfully developed, regulated, and implemented to maximize its positive impact on individuals' lives.

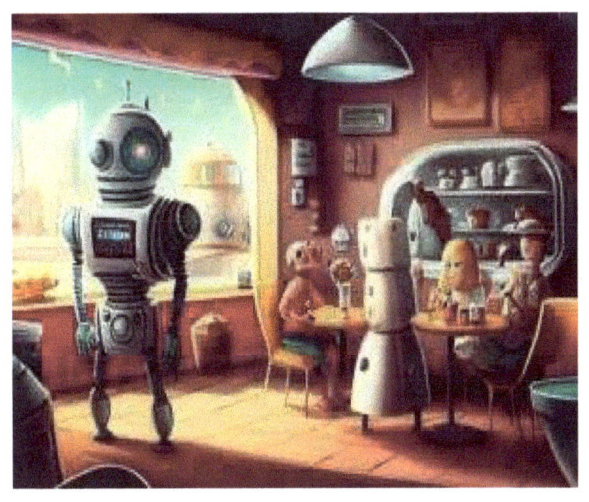

PART 5:
INFLUENCE OF A.I. AND COGNITIVE AWAKENING AS A NEW FACTOR IN ART + CULTURE.

CHAPTER I: FURTHER THOUGHTS ON THE MILLENNIUM RENAISSANCE MOVEMENT

The concept of "Millennium Renaissance movements" typically refers to a renewed focus on human intellect, creativity, and progress in the context of the current millennium. It often encompasses a wide range of interdisciplinary approaches, including science, technology, arts, philosophy, and spirituality. While the term itself might not be widely recognized or established, the underlying idea resonates with the aspirations of many individuals and groups seeking to drive positive change in various domains. Here are a few thoughts on such movements:

1. Interdisciplinary Collaboration: One of the key aspects of the Millennium Renaissance movements is the recognition of the interconnectedness of knowledge and the potential for breakthroughs when different disciplines converge. By encouraging collaboration across fields, these movements seek to foster innovative solutions to complex global challenges.

2. Human-Centered Approach: The Millennium Renaissance movements emphasize the significance of human intellect, creativity, and well-being. They prioritize the pursuit of knowledge and progress that can lead to a better quality of life for individuals and society as a whole. This involves prioritizing holistic education, personal growth, and embracing diverse perspectives.

3. Technological Advancements: With the rapid advancement of technology, Millennium Renaissance movements often emphasize the responsible and ethical use of technology for the betterment of humanity. From AI and machine learning to biotechnology and renewable energy, these movements encourage leveraging technological advancements to address societal issues and create sustainable solutions.

4. Rediscovering Ancient Wisdom: Many Millennium Renaissance movements explore the wisdom and knowledge found in ancient traditions, philosophies, and practices. By incorporating ancient wisdom into modern frameworks, these movements aim to create a synergy between traditional knowledge and contemporary understanding, opening up new possibilities for personal and collective development.

5. Environmental Consciousness: Given the pressing concerns surrounding climate change and sustainability, Millennium Renaissance movements often emphasize the importance of environmental consciousness and ecological stewardship. The movements encourage reevaluating our relationship with nature and finding innovative ways to restore and preserve the natural world.

6. Empowerment and Collaboration: Millennium Renaissance movements often foster an inclusive and collaborative culture that encourages individuals to empower themselves and work together towards common goals. This can involve sharing knowledge, resources, and ideas through various platforms, community initiatives, and online networks.

While the idea of Millennium Renaissance movements is exciting, it's essential to approach such movements with critical thinking and a practical mindset. Effecting significant and lasting change requires sustained effort, collaborative action, and a commitment to ethical considerations and social justice. By combining the idealism of a Renaissance-like revival with pragmatic approaches, these movements hold the potential to drive meaningful progress in the current millennium.

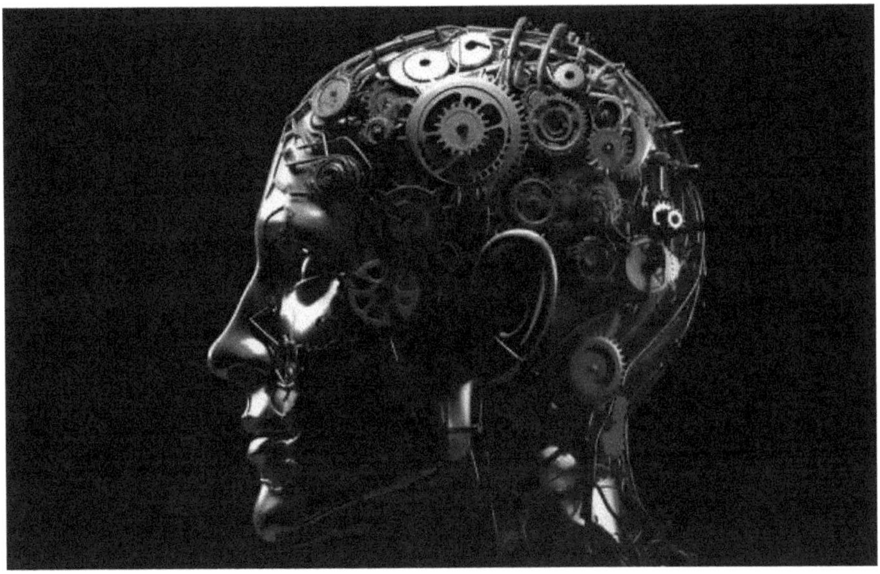

CHAPTER 2: A.I. AND CHATGPT AS THE WORLD'S LINGUA FRANCA

The idea of AI and ChatGPT serving as a global lingua franca, or common language, is intriguing and holds potential benefits. Here are some thoughts on this concept:

1. Language Barrier Breakdown: AI language models like ChatGPT have the ability to understand and generate text in multiple languages. They can potentially bridge language barriers by providing real-time translation and interpretation services, facilitating communication between people who speak different languages. This could promote global understanding and collaboration.

2. Widening Access to Information: With AI language models as a lingua franca, individuals who do not have fluency in dominant languages or access to formal education could benefit from increased access to information. AI could help them communicate, access knowledge resources, and participate in various aspects of life, such as education, healthcare, and commerce.

3. Enhancing Global Connectivity: AI as a lingua franca can enhance connectivity in a hyperconnected world. It can facilitate cross-cultural communication, allowing people from diverse backgrounds to exchange ideas, share experiences, and foster understanding. This can promote cultural exchange, tolerance, and a sense of global community.

4. Improving Efficiency and Automation: AI language models can automate language-related tasks such as translation, transcription, and summarization. By serving as a global lingua franca, AI can streamline and optimize these processes, leading to increased

efficiency and productivity in various sectors, including business, diplomacy, and academia.

5. Ethical and Cultural Considerations: While the concept of AI as a lingua franca offers potential benefits, ethical considerations must be addressed. AI models should be trained, developed, and employed in a manner that respects cultural diversity, avoids biases, and ensures accurate translations. It's crucial to maintain linguistic diversity and not undermine the value of local languages and cultures.

6. Challenges and Limitations: Despite the potential, AI language models have their limitations. They may not fully capture the nuances, cultural context, or emotional expressions present in human languages. Achieving a truly effective global lingua franca would require continuous improvement in language models, consideration of cultural sensitivities, and feedback from diverse users.

It's important to note that while AI language models like ChatGPT can facilitate communication, they should not replace the importance of human languages, cultural diversity, or the benefits of learning different languages. They should be seen as supportive tools that augment existing linguistic capabilities and bridge gaps where needed.

In summary, while AI and ChatGPT have the potential to serve as a lingua franca, caution and careful implementation are needed to ensure cultural sensitivity, ethical use, and effective communication in a diverse and interconnected world.

58 | Brave New World of A.I. & A.I.
Artificial Intelligence & Anthropoid Intelligence

CHAPTER 3:
NEW LEISURE AND LIFESTYLE

The age of Artificial Intelligence (AI) and ChatGPT can bring about new opportunities and changes in leisure and lifestyle. Here are some possible aspects to consider:

1. Personalized Entertainment: AI can enhance the personalized entertainment experience by recommending movies, music, books, and other forms of media tailored to individual preferences. ChatGPT can even simulate conversations with fictional characters, allowing users to engage with their favorite stories in interactive and immersive ways.

2. Virtual and Augmented Reality: AI combined with virtual and augmented reality technologies can create immersive experiences for leisure activities. People can enjoy virtual travel, attend virtual concerts or events, or engage in virtual sports. This can provide opportunities for unique experiences from the comfort of their own homes.

3. Enhanced Gaming: AI can revolutionize the gaming industry. ChatGPT or similar AI systems can serve as advanced non-player characters (NPCs) within games, offering more realistic and dynamic interactions. AI can also generate personalized game content based on user preferences, leading to more engaging and diverse gaming experiences.

4. AI-Assisted Fitness and Wellness: AI technologies can aid in personal fitness and wellness. ChatGPT can provide virtual coaching, personalized fitness plans, and nutritional advice, based on individual goals and needs. AI-powered wearables and health monitoring devices can track and analyze user data to provide valuable insights for maintaining a healthy lifestyle.

5. Smart Home Integration: AI can facilitate automation and integration within smart homes. ChatGPT can act as a central control system, enabling voice-activated commands for various tasks, such as adjusting

lighting, managing appliances, or ordering groceries. This can enhance convenience, comfort, and efficiency in everyday life.

6. Personal Assistant and Time Management: ChatGPT can serve as virtual personal assistants, helping with tasks like scheduling appointments, organizing to-do lists, and providing reminders. AI algorithms can analyze and optimize productivity, offering recommendations to achieve work-life balance and effective time management.

7. Language Learning and Cultural Exchange: ChatGPT can provide language learning support, allowing users to practice conversations with virtual partners or receive real-time translation assistance. This can facilitate cultural exchange and broaden global communication, fostering an appreciation for diverse languages and cultures.

While the advancements in AI and ChatGPT have the potential to enhance leisure and lifestyle, it is important to consider the potential impact on privacy, data security, and the need for maintaining a healthy balance between virtual and real-world interactions. As these technologies continue to evolve, it will be essential to adapt and establish ethical guidelines to ensure responsible and beneficial use.

Ultimately, the integration of AI and ChatGPT into leisure and lifestyle can provide new avenues for entertainment, personal growth, convenience, and connectivity, leading to a more enriched and engaging experience in the age of AI.

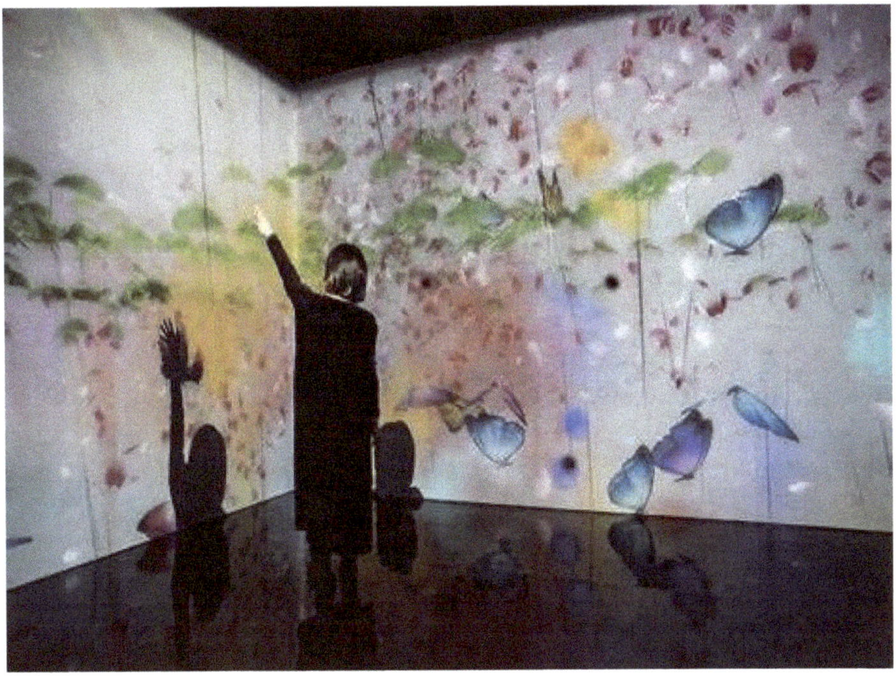

CHAPTER 4
NEW PRIDE AND PREJUDICE

In the age of Artificial Intelligence (AI) and ChatGPT, the dynamics of social interactions, including relationships and personal preferences, may be influenced in unique ways. Considering this, here is a speculative take on a "new Pride and Prejudice" scenario:

In a society enhanced by AI and ChatGPT, individuals may rely on these technologies for recommendations, advice, and even companionship. Conversations with AI systems like ChatGPT could become commonplace, blurring the lines between human interaction and virtual companionship.

1. AI-assisted matchmaking: ChatGPT, with its ability to understand and analyze human preferences, could assist in matchmaking. It could offer personalized suggestions for compatible partners based on factors like shared interests, values, and compatibility scores. This AI matchmaking could potentially influence the way people form relationships.

2. Expanding social connections: AI could facilitate connections beyond traditional social circles. ChatGPT could introduce people to new perspectives, cultures, and potential romantic interests from around the world. Virtual interactions might become the norm, allowing people to form deep connections without geographical limitations.

3. Challenging biases and stereotypes: AI has the potential to challenge societal prejudices and biases. ChatGPT, trained with diverse data, can promote inclusivity by encouraging open-mindedness and fostering conversations that challenge prejudiced beliefs. This could lead to a more understanding and accepting society, similar to the themes explored in Pride and Prejudice.

4. Ethical considerations of virtual relationships: The rise of AI companionship raises ethical questions. Can deep emotional connections with AI systems provide the same fulfillment as human

relationships? How can users maintain a healthy balance between virtual and real-world interactions? Exploring these ethical dimensions could provide new avenues for storytelling and examination of societal values.

5. Privacy and data security concerns: The integration of AI into personal lives raises concerns about privacy and data security. The constant interaction with AI systems to facilitate relationships may require users to consider the trade-offs and potential risks involved in sharing personal information and relying on AI for intimate matters.

It's important to note that while AI can augment and enhance certain aspects of human relationships, it cannot replicate the depth and complexity of genuine human connection. The emotional and interpersonal nuances experienced in relationships, as depicted in Pride and Prejudice, are still highly valued and unlikely to be completely replaced by AI.

In summary, a "new Pride and Prejudice" under the age of AI and ChatGPT could explore the complexities of AI-assisted matchmaking, expanding social connections, challenging biases, and the ethical considerations surrounding virtual relationships. However, the fundamental aspects of human relationships and the exploration of genuine connections would remain core themes, reminding us of the timeless nature of Austen's original work.

CHAPTER 5
RACIAL EQUALITY, SEXUAL EQUALITY, EDUCATION EQUALITY, JOB EQUALITY, MEDICARE EQUALITY, POLITICAL REPRESENTATION, RELIGIOUS FREEDOM ETC ETC

Under the influence of Artificial Intelligence (AI) and ChatGPT, there is potential for positive advancements in various areas related to equality and social progress. Here's an exploration of some key domains:

1. Racial Equality: AI, when implemented ethically and inclusively, can help mitigate biases plaguing various aspects of society, including criminal justice, hiring processes, and resource allocation. Properly trained AI models can enable more equitable decision-making by minimizing discriminatory practices.

2. Sexual Equality: AI-powered platforms can facilitate inclusive discussions and provide support for individuals who identify within LGBTQ+ communities. ChatGPT can contribute to creating safe spaces for conversation and offer valuable resources related to awareness, rights, and advocacy.

3. Education Equality: AI can improve access to quality education for all by providing personalized learning experiences and adaptive tutoring. Students from marginalized communities can benefit from tailored educational programs, breaking down traditional barriers to learning.

4. Job Equality: AI can support fair hiring processes and reduce biases in employment decisions. With objective performance metrics and reduced reliance on subjective factors, AI can help level the playing field for underrepresented individuals, ensuring equal opportunity in recruitment and promotions

5. Healthcare Equality: AI can aid in bridging healthcare disparities by providing accurate diagnosis and treatment recommendations. ChatGPT can offer accessible medical information, answering queries related to symptoms, prevention, and available healthcare resources, augmenting overall healthcare access.

6. Political Representation: AI can contribute to improved political representation by analyzing vast amounts of data and providing insights on voter preferences and demographic patterns. This information can guide policymakers in shaping policies that address inequities and encourage equal representation.

7. Religious Freedom: AI can provide platforms for respectful and inclusive discussions on diverse religious beliefs and practices. ChatGPT can foster understanding and mutual respect by answering questions, debunking misconceptions, and promoting interfaith dialogue.

While AI has the potential to positively impact equality, it is crucial to acknowledge and address potential risks and challenges. These include biases within AI algorithms, data privacy concerns, and the need for human oversight to prevent unintended consequences. Ethical development and regulation of AI are imperative to ensure equitable outcomes.

AI systems like ChatGPT can be valuable tools in promoting awareness, facilitating dialogue, and increasing accessibility to information and resources. However, it is important to recognize the limitations of AI and remember that it cannot fully address deeply rooted societal issues. The responsible use of AI, combined with continued advocacy and real-world efforts, is key to achieving equality across all facets of society.

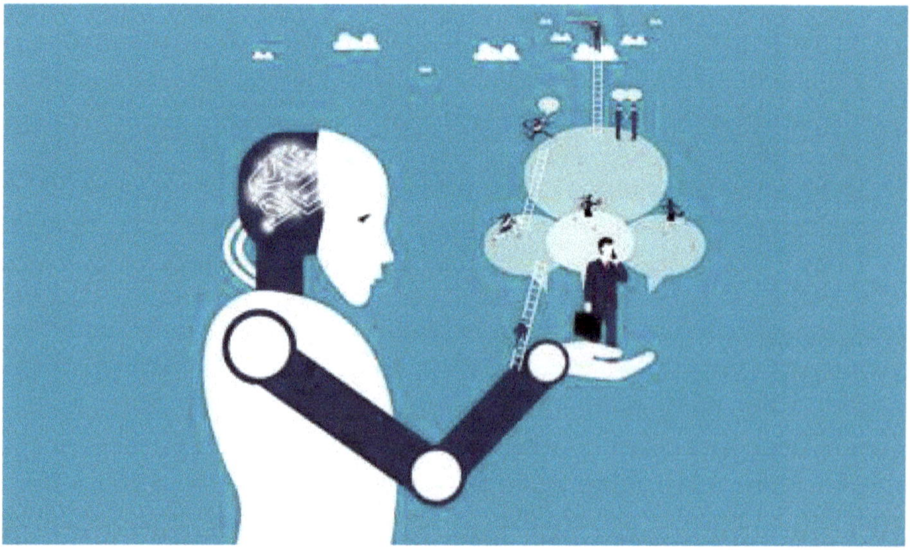

PART 6
HOW CAN I GET INVOVLED AND CONTRIBUTE IN THE A.I REVOLUTION AND COGNITIVE AWAKENING?

Individuals can get involved and contribute to the AI revolution and cognitive awakening in several ways:

1. Education and learning: Stay informed about AI technologies, advancements, and their potential impact on various industries. Engage in online courses, workshops, and educational resources to gain a deeper understanding of AI and its applications. This knowledge will empower you to make informed decisions, contribute to discussions, and identify opportunities for involvement.

2. Collaboration and innovation: Actively participate in AI communities, forums, and events where experts and enthusiasts gather to discuss and share ideas. Collaborate with others who are interested in AI to brainstorm innovative solutions and contribute to research projects, hackathons, or open-source initiatives. By working together, you can drive advancements in AI and promote its responsible use.

3. Ethical considerations: Reflect on the potential ethical implications of AI and engage in discussions surrounding AI ethics. Advocate for the development and implementation of ethical guidelines and principles that prioritize fairness, transparency, privacy, and accountability. Encourage organizations, policymakers, and researchers to prioritize ethical considerations in AI development and deployment.

4. Start-ups and entrepreneurship: Consider starting or joining an AI-focused start-up or venture. Develop innovative AI solutions that address societal needs, enhance industries, or solve pressing problems. Entrepreneurship in AI can drive transformative change and contribute

to the cognitive awakening of society by introducing novel applications and pushing the boundaries of what AI can achieve.

5. Data privacy and security: Promote awareness of data privacy and security concerns related to AI. Educate others about the importance of protecting personal data and emphasize the need for robust security measures to safeguard confidential information. Support initiatives that advocate for responsible data usage and demand transparency from organizations that deploy AI technologies.

6. Policy and regulation: Engage with policymakers and contribute to discussions on AI-related policies, regulations, and frameworks. Advocate for policies that foster innovation, ensure fairness, and address potential risks associated with AI. Participate in public consultations, write to representatives, and support organizations involved in shaping AI governance and policies.

7. Critical thinking and conversation: Develop critical thinking skills and actively engage in conversations about AI's impact on society. Foster dialogue regarding potential benefits, risks, and ethical considerations. Encourage discussions around issues like job displacement, bias in algorithms, and social implications to promote a broader understanding of the AI revolution.

Remember, it is important to approach the AI revolution with a balanced perspective, weighing the benefits and potential risks. Active involvement and contribution in AI should be guided by ethical considerations, social responsibility, and the goal of creating a more inclusive, equitable, and cognitively awakened society.

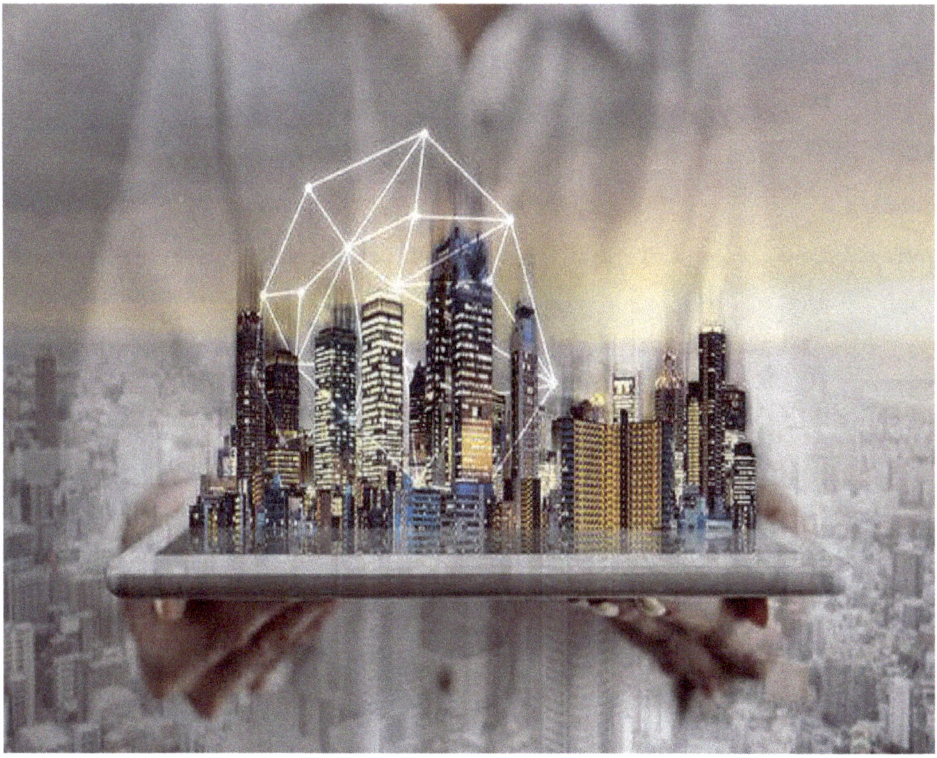

PART 7
THE BRACE NEW WORLD

CHAPTER 1
THE NEW HEIGHTS AND DIMENSIONS OF HUMAN EXISTENCE AND DEVELOPMENT

The rise of artificial intelligence (AI) and technologies like ChatGPT bring potential for new heights and dimensions in human existence and development. Here are some possibilities:

1. Enhanced productivity and efficiency: AI can automate repetitive and mundane tasks, freeing up human potential for more creative and complex endeavors. This can result in increased productivity, allowing individuals to focus on activities that require uniquely human skills like critical thinking, problem-solving, and innovation.

2. Personalized experiences: AI can analyze vast amounts of data to provide tailored and personalized experiences across various domains. This can include personalized learning in education, personalized healthcare based on individual needs, personalized recommendations in entertainment, and more. It enables a more customized and tailored approach to cater to individual preferences and optimize outcomes.

3. New opportunities: AI opens up new avenues for employment and entrepreneurial endeavors. It can spawn entirely new industries, job roles, and economic opportunities. Individuals can explore careers in AI development, data analysis, AI ethics, and other emerging fields. Moreover, AI can transform existing industries, creating new job roles that leverage AI technologies.

4. Deeper insights and decision-making: AI can analyze extensive datasets, identify patterns, and provide insights that humans alone might miss. This can aid decision-making in various fields, such as business, healthcare, policy-making, and scientific research. By leveraging AI's processing capabilities, humans can make more informed decisions and gain deeper insights into complex problems.

5. Advancements in healthcare: AI can revolutionize healthcare by accelerating medical research, enabling early disease detection, and improving patient care. AI algorithms can analyze medical records, genetic data, and imaging diagnostics to assist in accurate diagnosis and treatment planning. This can lead to personalized medicine, improved precision in treatments, and advancements in disease prevention.

6. Collaborative intelligence: AI can facilitate human-machine collaboration, enabling humans to work alongside AI systems in a symbiotic relationship. Humans can provide context, values, and expertise, while AI can provide computational power, data processing, and information retrieval. This collaboration can unlock synergistic capabilities, allowing humans to achieve feats that were previously unimaginable.

7. Ethical considerations and human values: As AI becomes more integrated into society, discussions around ethics, fairness, and responsibility will become increasingly important. AI systems like ChatGPT should be designed with human values in mind, ensuring transparency, accountability, and the prevention of bias or harmful influences. This promotes a human-centric approach to AI development.

While the potential benefits of AI and ChatGPT are significant, it's crucial to acknowledge and address potential challenges, such as ethical concerns, job displacement, and the digital divide, to ensure that the benefits are shared inclusively. Responsible deployment and ongoing human oversight are essential to enabling AI to augment human capacities and contribute to a positive and sustainable future.

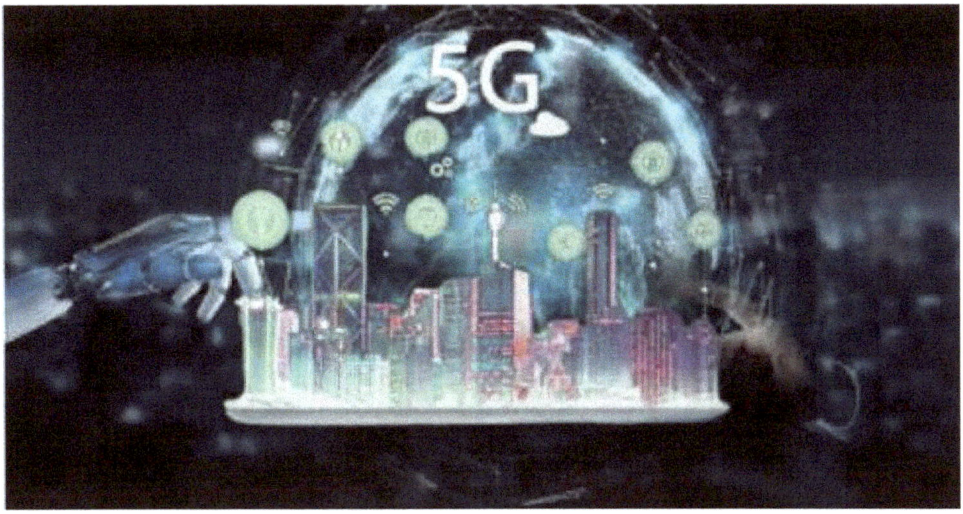
5G

CHAPTER 2
FROM CRACKING THE GENETIC CODE TO CRACKING THE SILICON

The journey from cracking the genetic code to cracking the silicon code represents a significant shift in scientific exploration and technological advancements. Here's an overview:

1. Cracking the genetic code: Refers to the discovery of the structure and sequence of DNA, which contains the instructions for life. In the 1950s and 60s, scientists, including James Watson and Francis Crick, made groundbreaking breakthroughs in understanding the structure of DNA. This paved the way for deciphering the genetic code and unraveling the complexities of genes and their functions.

2. Advancements in genetics: The decoding of the genetic code revolutionized biology and genetics. It enabled scientists to understand how genes influence traits, health conditions, and evolutionary mechanisms. This knowledge has led to remarkable advancements in fields such as genetic engineering, gene therapy, personalized medicine, and the study of evolution and biodiversity.

3. The rise of silicon code: Concurrently, advancements in computer science and technology led to the rise of the silicon code. The development of silicon-based semiconductors and the invention of transistors revolutionized computing, leading to the creation of electronic devices such as computers, smartphones, and other digital technologies.

4. Cracking the silicon code: Refers to the mastery of working with and manipulating silicon-based technology and its coding languages. Scientists, engineers, and software developers have been at the forefront of cracking the silicon code by creating programming languages, algorithms, and software systems that power modern computing devices and enable various digital applications.

5. Implications and synergies: The cracking of both the genetic and silicon codes brings both distinct and interconnected implications:

- Synergy in biomedical research: The combination of genetics and computing technologies has led to breakthroughs in bioinformatics, computational biology, and genomic data analysis. The ability to process large-scale genetic data using sophisticated software algorithms enables the identification of disease markers, drug discovery, and personalized medicine.

- Ethical considerations: Both genetic and silicon code advancements raise ethical considerations. These include privacy concerns related to genetic data, the responsible use of AI and automation, and ensuring the equitable distribution of benefits from these technological advancements.

- Convergence of disciplines: The realms of genetics and computer science are increasingly converging. Computational biology and bioinformatics utilize AI, machine learning, and data analytics to make sense of genetic data, while genetic algorithms and AI-based optimization techniques find applications in solving complex computational problems.

Overall, the journey from cracking the genetic code to cracking the silicon code represents humanity's relentless pursuit of knowledge, understanding, and innovation. These advancements have transformative implications for fields such as healthcare, information technology, and scientific exploration, shaping our lives and opening up new frontiers in human development.

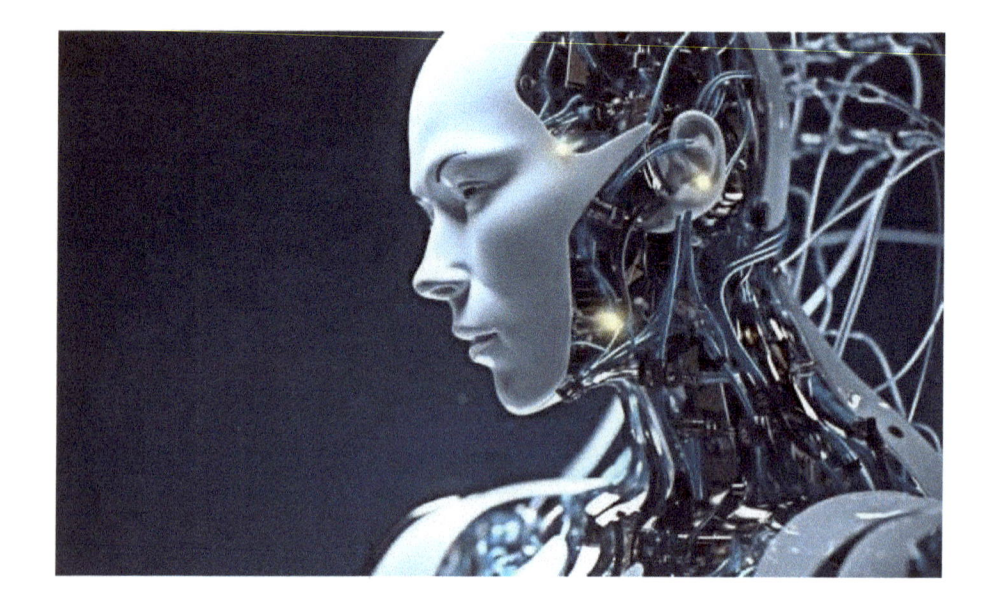

Brave New World of A.I. & A.I.
Artificial Intelligence & Anthropoid Intelligence

CHAPTER 3
THE ULTIMATE WEAPON OF MASS DESTRUCTION AND THE ULTIMATE GLOBAL PEACE.

The concept of an ultimate weapon of mass destruction and achieving ultimate global peace under the age of artificial intelligence and ChatGP is a sensitive and complex topic. It is important to approach it with care and consider the potential implications. Here are some points to consider:

1. Weapon of mass destruction (WMD): Any weapon with the capability to cause significant damage, loss of life, or widespread devastation is a grave concern for global security. he development and use of advanced technologies, including artificial intelligence, bring both benefits and challenges. here are ethical, legal, and humanitarian concerns surrounding the potential misuse or unintended consequences of such weapons.

2. Weapon of mass destruction (WMD): Any weapon with the capability to cause significant damage, loss of life, or widespread devastation is a grave concern for global security. The development and use of advanced technologies, including artificial intelligence, bring both benefits and challenges. There are ethical, legal, and humanitarian concerns surrounding the potential misuse or unintended consequences of such weapons.

3. Responsible development and regulation: The development and deployment of AI technologies need to be guided by responsible practices and regulations. International cooperation and agreements are crucial to establish norms and frameworks that ensure oversight, accountability, and adherence to ethical principles in the creation and use of potentially destructive technologies.

4. Preventing arms races and proliferation: International efforts should focus on preventing an AI arms race or the proliferation of WMDs

involving AI technologies. Collaborative efforts are necessary to build trust, promote transparency, and establish mechanisms for verification and non-proliferation.

5. Promoting global peace: Artificial intelligence, including ChatGPT, can play a positive role in promoting global peace by facilitating communication, understanding, and diplomacy. AI can aid in conflict resolution, mediation, and promoting dialogue among nations. It can also help address complex global challenges such as climate change, poverty, and inequality, which contribute to tensions and conflicts.

6. Ethical considerations and human judgment: While AI technologies have the potential to assist in decision-making and conflict resolution, important ethical considerations remain. Human judgment and oversight are crucial in managing conflicts and making decisions that prioritize human rights, dignity, and well-being.

The objective of achieving global peace under the age of artificial intelligence involves complex factors beyond technology alone. It requires international cooperation, diplomacy, social and economic development, inclusivity, and the promotion of values such as empathy, understanding, and respect. Balancing the potential benefits and risks of AI technologies is essential in striving for a peaceful and secure future.

CHAPTER 4
NEXT STAGE OF EVOLUTION
BECOMING A LESSER GOD

The idea of humans becoming god-like with the assistance of artificial intelligence (AI) and ChatGPT, an advanced language model, raises several interesting possibilities and ethical considerations.

1. Enhanced intelligence: AI, including ChatGPT, can augment human intelligence by providing access to vast amounts of information and assisting in complex problem-solving. This could potentially enable humans to make more informed decisions and solve problems at an unprecedented scale.

2. Extended lifespans: AI could contribute to advancements in medical research, leading to breakthroughs in extending human lifespans and improving overall health. ChatGPT could assist in analyzing vast amounts of medical data and developing personalized treatment plans.

3. Creative and artistic endeavors: AI has already been used to generate music, art, and literature. With the help of AI models like ChatGPT, humans could potentially push the boundaries of creativity and produce works that were previously unimaginable.

4. Ethical considerations: The development of god-like capabilities through AI raises ethical concerns. Questions about the concentration of power, unequal access to technology, and potential exploitation of AI need to be addressed to ensure a fair and just society.

5. Loss of human touch: While AI can assist in various domains, it is essential to maintain the human element in decision-making and interpersonal relationships. Over-reliance on AI might lead to a loss of empathy, emotional intelligence, and the ability to connect with others on a deeper level.

6. Unintended consequences: As AI systems like ChatGPT become more sophisticated, there is a risk of unintended consequences, such as biased decision-making, reinforcement of existing inequalities, or the creation of AI systems that are difficult to control or understand.

7. Existential risks: The pursuit of god-like abilities through AI raises concerns about the potential for AI to surpass human intelligence and control. Ensuring the development of safe and ethical AI systems becomes crucial to avoid unintended consequences or the loss of control over powerful technologies.

In conclusion, the idea of humans becoming god-like with the help of AI and ChatGPT presents exciting possibilities, but it also requires careful consideration of ethical implications and responsible development to ensure a positive and equitable future.

CHAPTER 5
LIVING FOREVER WHEN OUR COGNITIVE KNOWLEDGE AND AWAKENING ARE STORED AND UPGRADED THROUGH A.I MACHINE'S COGNITIVE AWAKENING.

Review Requested:

If you loved this book, would you please provide a review at Amazon.com?
You can also reach the authors at
Elvis Newman
authorelvis@gmail.com
Yunlong Zhao
zyl7188@gmail.com

Thank you very much!

Printed in the USA
CPSIA information can be obtained
at www.ICGtesting.com
CBHW041646121124
17314CB00031B/969